Their Majesties, King and Queen of Bhutan

ブータンを「江戸時代」と表現した人がいる。「タイム・スリップしたみたい」という人もいる。それくらい手つかずの自然があり、文明的なものがほとんどない。そんなブータンに世界最高級レベルの快適なリゾートホテルがある。それも、手つかずの自然と調和するように工夫されたものが…。コモ・グループが運営する2つの「ウマ・バイ・コモ」（Uma BY COMO）だ。ブータン唯一の国際空港があるパロ（Paro）と、パロから車で約4時間移動する古都プナカ（Punakha）とにある。古都プナカに2012年に出来た「ウマ・バイ・コモ、プナカ」（Uma BY COMO, Punakha）は、プナカ谷のモチュウ川（母川の意）に沿って建てられ、ブータンならでは田園風景に囲まれている。「世界中のリゾートには一通り行った」という人でも退屈しない最高のリゾートだ。ブータンへの入国はビザが必要で事前に現地旅行代理店を通じて取得する必要がある。また、インド等を除く外国人旅行者には1日あたり200～290米ドルの旅費（いわゆる公定料金。人数・時期による）を要求される。手続きは一見面倒そうだが、すべてウマでやってくれる。ブータンに旅行したくなったときに必要なのは、ウマにメールすることだけだ。

When you are in Bhutan, you may feel as if you have time-travelled to the world 300 years ago, because it is difficult to find civilized things like buildings and paved roads. You see the rural landscape only. Uma BY COMO, however, provides the two world class resorts in Bhutan, one in Paro, whiich has the sole international airport, and another in Punakha, the old capital of the country. "Uma BY COMO, Punakha", situated on a bend in the Mo Chu river in Punakha Valley, is an exciting destination for those who have visited most famous resorts all over the world and are looking for something new. In order to visit Bhutan, you need to obtain a visa piror to the visit, and there are special regulations about the minimum daily fare and daily government tax for foreigners. Though it sounds complicated, you only need to contact "Uma" and they will arrange all the necessary details. Just e-mail to Uma whenever you want to visit Bhutan.

外観はブータン風
The exterior of the resort looks Bhutanese.

気持ちの良いテラス
Refreshing air on the terrace.

地元のオーガニックの食材はシンプルな料理で引き立つ
Simple dishes made from local organic foods are very tasty.

プナカはブータンの昔の首都だが、人口もわずか7000人。日本の感覚で言うと、「首都」というよりも「村」だ。「ウマ・バイ・コモ・プナカ」はそのはずれにある。外観も内装もブータン風だが、設備が整った快適なリゾートだ。食亭は地元のオーガニックな食材で作られる。食べるだけでリフレッシュされる感覚がある。

Punakha was the capital of Bhutana until 1955, but the population is just 7,000 people. Uma BY COMO is located there. The exterior and interior is very Bhutanise, but, at the same time, it has very modern equipments, too. The dishes served there are made from local organic produce. You will be refreshed just by eating the food.

木の香りが心地よいロビー
Lobby area with the comfortable smell of wood.

暖炉
A fireplace in the lobby area

タシタゲと呼ばれる吉祥紋の模様
Tashitage, a happy motif in Tibetan Buddhism

普段、先進国で生活する人には、これだけ静かで落ち着いた夜を経験することは珍しい体験だろう。とにかく静かなのだ。風の音、水のせせらぎ、動物の声など、自然の音以外は何も聞こえない。現地の木材で作られたロビーには暖炉があり、タシタゲと呼ばれるチベット仏教特有の吉祥紋が描かれた装飾品がエキゾチックに並ぶ。

I am sure you, who lives in modern cities, will find the quite nights a unique experience. There are only the natural sounds like wind, water, and animal's voices. The lobby area, built with local wood, has a fireplace and also have many cheeful motifs inTibetan Buddhism, called "Tashitage".

客室からは、大きな窓を通して幻想的な自然の景色が広がる。客室も、その景色に会ったシンプルで暖かい内装だ。もちろん設備は最新のものが完備しているので非常に快適だ。Us hem hae adem pati,

You will enjoy the natural view from the guest room through large windows. The interior of the bedrooms matches the view. The eqiupment is modern so the stay is very comfortable.

室内の大きな窓からプナカ谷を一望できる。
You can enjoy the view of Punakha Valley from the room.

このマークがリゾートの目印だ
This logo is the trademark for the resort

ベッドルームはシンプルで寝心地がよい。
The comfortable bedroom gives you a good sleep.

Uma BY COMO, Punakha

URL : www.comohotels.com/umapunakha

E-mail : res.uma.punakha@comohotels.com

Tel : +975 2 584 688

Rates 料金：Valley View Room US$ 550~ (Subject to changes)
+10% Tax and 10% Service Charge　10％税＋10％サービス料　別
including breakfast and dinner for two (excluding bevalraes) 朝食夕食込（飲み物は別料金）

How to get there : About 4 hours drive from Paro International airport,
行き方：ブータン唯一の国際空港であるパロ国際空港から車で約4時間
* Paro International airport is the sole international airport in Bhutan.

ゾンはチベット語で「要塞」を意味する（ブータンの公用語はゾンカ語だが、チベット語の方言の一種だとされる。ちなみに英語が準公用語でブータン人は英語は堪能な人が多い）。ゾンは単なる要塞ではなく、寺院、修道院、行政機関を持つ一種のコンプレックスだった。17世紀に建てられたプナカ・ゾンは、ウマ・プナカ（P2-P7）から車で約20分ほど。プナカの最大の観光地だ。ポチュー・リバー（父川）とモチュー・リバー（母川）の合流地点に立地する。2011年に、今のワンチュク国王（第5代ブータン国王）がペマ王妃と結婚式を挙げたのも、このプナカ・ゾンだった。プナカが古都であることは述べたが、第2代の国王の時代までは、このプナカ・ゾンに王国政府があった。

Dzong means "fortress" in Dzongka language, the public language in Bhutan, which is regarded as one of the dialects of Tibetan. (For your information, Bhutanese people speak good English and English is the semi-publuic language there.). Dzong was not only a fortress but also a kind of complex, with a temple, a monastery, and the governent office. Punakha Dzong was built in the 17th century and it takes about 20 minutes from Uma Phunaka (P2~P7). It is the most famous touristic place in Punakha and located at the confluence of th Po Chu river, "Father" river, and Mo Chu river, "Mother" river. The current King Wangchuk, the 5th King of Bhutan, and his wife, Queen consort Pema, had their wedding ceremony at this Punakha Dzong. Again, Punakha was the old capital of Bhutan, and until the reign of the 2nd King, Punakha Dzong had the kingdom's government.

ブータンの寺院には五色（青、白、赤、緑、黄）が必ずある。
Any temple in Bhutan has five-color prayer flags, blue, white, red, green and yellow.

マニ車。お経が書かれており、一回転させるとお経を一度読んだのと同じ功徳があるとされる。
Prayer wheel. Spinning it one time is regarded as a one-time reading of a suntra.

パロ国際空港から車で約10分のところに、「ウマ・バイ・コモ・パロ」(Uma BY COMO, Paro) がある。ブータンの高級リゾートブームの火付け役になった代表的なリゾートだ。現代的な施設と、ヒマラヤ・ブータンの伝統的な雰囲気がみごとに融合している。快適な滞在は請け合いだ。

Uma BY COMO, Paro, is located 10 minutes by car from Paro international airport. The resort is the one which sparked the boom of lusury resorts in Bhutan. The modern equipment is matched by the Himarayan Bhutanese tradition in the resort.

013

ここで絶対のお勧めはホット・ストーンバスだ。オーガニックのヨモギが浮いている浴槽の奥に熱く熱した石を入れることでお湯を適温にする。ぬるいときは、奥の木戸を叩くと石が追加される。

I strongly recommend you to take a "hot stone bath". There is a space to put heated hot stones in order to warm the water and mugwort leaves in the bathtub. When you want to make it warmer, you knock the small wood door and an addtional hot stone is dropped.

こんな具合だ。
It is like this.

ウマ・パロのレストラン
Restaurant in Uma Paro

食事もおいしい。お勧めはブータニーズ・セット（下表）だ。地元の人が食べる料理は、日本人には強烈に辛すぎて食べられないが、ここでは外国人向けにマイルドになっている。

The restaurant serves you delicious dishes. My recommendation is the "Bhutanese Set" for dinner. The real local foods are too spicy for foreigners, so the food here is milder to fit our tasktes. The menu of a "Bhutanese Set" on a one-off day is as follows.

"Bhutanese Set" on a day

*Local Buckwheat dumpling with radish, mustard green, local cheese & chilli dipping sauce （地元のそば団子、蕪・芥子菜・地元のチーズとチリソース添え）

*Nettle soup with local tofu （地元の豆腐入りイラクサのスープ）

*Sauteed greens with Sichuan pepper, garlic & chilli flake
（野菜の唐辛子・にんにく・たかの爪炒め）

*Braised local pork curry with radish & coriander (Left photo)
（蕪・コリアンダー入り、蒸し煮された地元の豚肉カレー。左の写真）

016

Uma BY COMO, Paro

URL :　www.comohotels.com/umaparo

E-mail : res.uma.paro@comohotels.com

Tel :　　+975 8 271 597

Rates 料金：Como Suite US$ 750~ (Subject to changes)

+10% Tax and 10% Service Charge　10％税＋10％サービス料　別
including breakfast and dinner for two (excluding bevalraes) 朝食夕食込（飲み物は別料金）

How to get there : Just 10 minutes drive from Paro Inernational airport.
行き方：ブータン唯一の国際空港であるパロ国際空港から車でわずか約10分
* Paro International airport is the sole international airport in Bhutan.

パロの町のど真ん中の光景。ブータンの大きな町と言えば、首都のティンプーと空港のあるパロ。ブータン料理に欠かせない唐辛子は至るところに干されている。
This is the center of Paro, which has the sole international airport in Bhutan. It is one of two towns in the country. The other, Thimphu, the capital. Even in the center of town, we easily come across many red peppers being dried.

村の祭りの光景。世界どこでもこれが子宝の象徴だ。
A scene of from a village festival. Anywhere in the world, this is a lucky simbol for virility.

これが、かの有名なタイガーズ・ネストだ。タクツァン僧院までのトレッキングもできる。
This is the famous "Tiger's Nest", which is home to the Taktsang Monastery. Treking up here is popular.

ブータン豆知識

◇1ブータンニュルタム＝1.7円（2014年3月現在）だが、インド・ルピーもそのまま使える。

◇ビザなどの手続きは複雑そうに見えるが、ここで紹介したリゾートは一連の手続きを代行してくれるので心配不要。

◇一般的なブータンへの行き方は、タイのバンコクで、ブータン国営航空ドゥルック航空あるいはタシ航空に乗り換え。

◇ブータン観光の情報は、ブータン政府観光局のウェブサイトでゲット。

http://www.travel-to-bhutan.jp/

Basic Information about Bhutan

* The currency in Bhutan is Bhutanese Ngultrum (BTN). 100 BTN = US$ 1.64 (as of March 2014). Indian Rupee can be used in Bhutan, too.

* Though The process to obtain visa looks complicated, you just need to e-mail the resorts introduced here. They will look ater everything for you.

* To get there, you transit at Bangkog, Thailand, to Drukair, the national airline of Bhutan, or Bhutan Airlines, a new private airline.

* Tourism information is avaialbe at :
    http://www.tourism.gov.bt/

Metropolitan by COMO, Bangkok

メトロポリタン・バイ・コモ・バンコク（以下、メトロポリタン）は、バンコクで有名なシーロム通と並行して走るサトーン通にある。サトーン通は金融機関・一流企業のオフィスのみならず、5つ星ホテルが立ち並ぶ。スワンナプーム国際空港から車で1時間弱だ。
Metropolitan by COMO, Bangkok is located along Sathorn Road, which has not only banks and offices but also many 5-star hotels. It takes less than one hour from Suvarnabhumi International Airport.

メトロポリタン・バイ・コモ・バンコク（以下、メトロポリタン）は、喧騒とは無縁の快適な滞在が楽しめる。
You enjoy the stay at Metropolitan by COMO, Bangkok, without noise and chaos of the city.

初めてのバンコク滞在なら、ホテルは有名なマンダリン・オリエンタルでもいいかもしれない。だが、二度目以降で落ち着いて過ごしたいときには、このメトロポリタンが最高だ。

If it's your first trip to Bangkok, the choice for accomodation may be the Mandarin Oriental. If this is your second time or more, there's no doubt you would stay at Metropolitan by COMO, Bangkok.

021

洗練された内装の広い部屋。The rooms are wide with sophisticatd interior.

バンコクと言えば、ワットポーなどでアクロバティックなタイマッサージを楽しんでもらいたいが、メトロポリタン内の「コモ・シャンバラ」という世界トップクラスのスパで、ゆっくりとセラピーを楽しむことをお勧めする。英語では COMO Shambhala Urban Escape と表記されるが、その名のとおり、都会の忙しい生活から「逃避」でき、ストレスが身体から抜けるのを実感できるだろう。左の写真のジャグジーを見るだけでリラックスできるのではないだろうか。

　また、屋外には20ｍプールがあり、プールサイドのデッキチェアでは日光浴も楽しめる。

Y ou may enjoy Thai Massage at Wat Pho in Bangkok, a Buddhist temple in Phra Nakhon district, where the massage school and its massage clinic is very famous and popular.

　At the same time, I recommend you to have the world-top-class SPA therapies at COMO Shambhala Urban Escape, the luxury SPA in Metropolitan. I am sure that you will feel that the stress from your daily life is gone. Look at the above photo of jacuzzi, the sight of which alone, I think, gives you a feeling of relaxation.

　Metroplitan also has a 20 meter outdoor swimming pool, where you get a tan on a deck.

メトロポリタンには「ナーム（nahm）」というタイ料理のレストランがある。レストランマガジンという英国雑誌で、2014年の世界のベスト・レストラン第13位、アジアのベスト・レストラン50の第1位に選ばれている。現地では予約が困難なレストランとして知られている。宿泊予約と同時に予約することをお勧めする。
Metropolitan has a famous Thai restaurant "nahm", which has received a wonderful award in 2014 by a UK magazine "Restaurant Magazine", TOP13 in World's Best 50 Restaurantts and NO.1 in Asia's Best 50 Restaurants.

ナームの「ピーナッツのオードブル、グリルしたエビ添え」
"Peanut Relish with Grilled Prawns" served by nahm
Metropolitan by COMO, Bangkok

025

メトロポリタンは、数日の滞在なら、ホテルの中で十分楽しめるくらい充実している。たとえば、MetBAR（メット・バー）。ロンドンにあるメット・バー同様、ホテルの宿泊客を除くとメンバーだけが利用できる特別なバーだ。地元のセレブご用達らしい。また、ナーム以外の、もう一つのレストランGlow（グロー）は、身体に良いナチュラルでオーガニックな素材を生かしたヘルシーな料理を提供する。ホテルでの朝食はグローで食べることができる。日本からブータン（P1〜）へはバンコク乗り換えが典型的だが、その乗り継ぎ時の滞在に最適だ。

The other places in Metropolitan are also enjoyable. For example, Met BAR is a very special bar where only members and hotel guests can visit, same as Met BAR in London. The local celebrities love to go there. There is another restaurant, apart from "nahm", named "Glow". It serves healthy dishes with natual and organic produce. The hotel guests have breakfast at Glow. Metropolitan is the best hotel for transit from Tokyo to Bhutan, introduced from page 1.

Glow の料理はいつもフレッシュな味がする。
The dishes served at Glow always taste fresh.

Metropolitan by COMO, Bangkok

URL： www.comohotels.com/metropolitanbangkok
E-mail : met.bkk@comohotels.com
Tel： +66 2 625 3333
Rates 料金： City room (30 sq.m) THB8,500 (Subject to changes)
＊シティ・ルームは日本円で約 27,000 円（＋税・サ別）
（1 TBH（タイ・バーツ）＝約3.2円（2014年5月1日現在）で計算
＊ +7% VAT and 10% Service Charge 7% 税＋ 10% サービス料 別

マカティは、フィリピンの首都マニラの金融経済の中心地だ。東京の丸の内、大手町に相当するエリア。マカティのホテルと言えば、長い間、最もよいホテルはシャングリラ・マカティだと相場が決まっていた。しかし、2012年12月にラッフルズ・マカティがオープンしてからは事情が変わった。泊まってわかったが、個人的にはラッフルズ・マカティの方が圧倒的に快適だと思う。まず、部屋が広い。ホテルの客室は全室スイートルームで、32室しかない。一番狭いジュニア・スイートでも60平米もある。一人あるいは二人で泊まるには十分な広さだ。また、雰囲気が明るい。客室の淡い色の内装や大きな窓のせいだろう。やわらかい色調で明るさに満ち溢れている。装飾品もユニークだ。現代的なアートがふんだんに使われている。とにかく素晴らしいの一言に尽きる。

Makati is the center of financial and economic activity in Manila, the capital city of Philippines. It is equivalent to Marunouchi or Otemachi area in Tokyo. The best hotel in Makati had been Shangri-la Makati for a long time. After Raffles Makati opened in December 2012, the situation was changed. In my opinion, and I have experienced both hotels, Raffles Makati is much more comfortable. First, the rooms are larger. Raffles Makati has 32 rooms only, all suite rooms. The smallest room is Junior Suite, and even that measures 60 square meters. It is large enough for one or two persons to stay. The lobby and the rooms are full of light, because of the light color of the interiors and the large floor-to-ceiling windows. And the hotel has many modern art works. Just one word: Awesome!

寝　心地のよいベッド、深いバスタブなど、日本人も満足すること請け合いだ。最近は外国人でも、セレブは深いバスタブに浸かることを好むらしいが。また、屋外のプールや、ウィロー・ストリーム・スパという名前のスパも充実している。

I am veru sure that even Japanese people will be satisfied with its comfortable and wide beds and deep bathtubs. As you may know, taking a bath in a bathtub is a kind of necessary for Japanese people. Showers are not enough for them. A better thing than that is a bathtub that is deep. Raffles Makati has a good spa called Willow Stream Spa and an outdoor swimming pool as well.

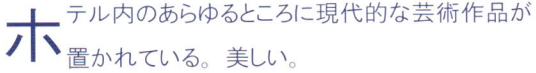

ホ テル内のあらゆるところに現代的な芸術作品が
　 置かれている。美しい。
R affles Makati has many modern art works
　inside. They are very beautiful.

031

ロング・バーの長いカウンター
The long counter at Long Bar

ラッフルズ・マカティはダイニングも充実している。朝食はオープンキッチンのスペクトラム（Spectrum）。アフタヌーンティー（写真P33）はライターズ・バー（Writer's Bar）。何よりもリラックスできるロング・バー（Long Bar）。長いカウンターとオリジナルカクテルが特徴的だ。

Dining in Raffles Makati is also wonderful. You enjoy breakfast at Spectrum, with an open kitchen. Afternoon Tea is served at Writer's Bar. I like Long Bar, famous for its long counter and original cocktails, because I can really relux with the nostalgic atmosphere.

032

ライターズ・バーのアフタヌーン・ティー
Afternoon Tea at Writer's Bar

Raffles Makati
URL： www.raffles.com/makati/
E-mail： concierge.makati@raffles.com
Tel： +632 555 9777
Rates 料金：**Junior Suite (60 sq.m) PHP15,300** (Subject to changes)
＊ジュニア・スイートは日本円で約 35,000 円（＋税・サ別）
　（1 PHP (Philippine Peso)＝約 2.3 円（2014年5月1日現在）で計算
＊ **+12.6% government tax and 10% Service Charge** 12.6% 税＋ 10% サービス料 別

残念なことに、フィリピンに存在するというだけで世界一流の洗練されたリゾートとは思われないかもしれない。しかし、前に紹介したラッフルズ・マカティ（P28〜）といい、このザ・ファーム・アット・サン・ベニート（以下、単に「ザ・ファーム」）といい、世界のどこの高級リゾートと比較してもまったく引けを取らないリゾートが今やフィリピンにもある。私が感じた、このザ・ファームの特徴は、①自然の中にあり鈍感な私でもマイナスイオンを感じる、②食事が非常にヘルシー。肉・魚を使わないが満足できる、③部屋の設備は非常に近代的、④他のアクティビィティも充実していて退屈しない、の4点だ。マニラのニノイ・アキノ国際空港から約1時間強で着くから、日本からはかなり近い。

You may think that resorts in Philippines would not be so sophisticated as the first class resorts in other parts of the world. But that's wrong now. I am sure that THE FARM AT SAN BENITO ("THE FARM") is one of the best health conscious resorts in the world. The reasons: 1) Surrounded by greenery with fresh air, 2)Healthy food wihtout meat and fish, but satisfying nonetheless. 3) The inside of the rooms are modern. and 4)You cannot get bored with many health-related activities on offer. From Japan, it is very close. Just over an hour's car drive brings you to the resort from Ninoy Aquino International Airport in Manila.

敷地内で取れる野菜や果物のおいしさを味わってほしい
You will find how delicious the fresh fruits and vegetables grown in the resort area.

味付けはしっかりしているし、ナッツ類もあるので満足感は得られる。
たとえば右下は、ベーコンに見えても「もどき」だ。
The seasoning of the dishes are good and they use nuts in the dishes.
So you will be satisfied with the food even without meat and fish.
The bottom right photo looks like a bacon, but it is not.

037

リゾート内のクリニックでは白血球の様子を観察できる。いゆわる血がサラサラかの検査だ（右上写真）。
You can observe the situation of your white blood corpuscle (right photo) at a clinic in the resort.

ヨガもある。Yoga class may be in the morning. Afternoon is for the groups. Private yoga class can be arranged too.

料理教室もある。They have a "raw food preparation class".

リゾート内の、水に浮いた綺麗な花はスタッフが毎日新しく造る
The resort staff make the water floor arrangements, known as "Mandala Floral Arrangement", every day. It's another therapeutic activity.

039

客室（ナラビラ・スイート）にプライベート・プールがある。
室内のバスタブは大きく、ゆったりと入浴できる。

THE FARM AT SAN BENITO

URL : www.thefarmatsanbenito.com
Email : info@thefarm.com.ph ＊英語のみ
日本語で問い合わせは ah@thefarm.com.ph
Tel : +63 2 884 8074
Rates 料金：**Palmera Suites (39 sq.m) PHP14,700** (Subject to changes)

＊パルメラ・スイートは日本円で約33,800円（＋税・サ別）
（1 PHP (Philippine Peso)＝約2.3円（2014年5月1日現在）で計算
＊ +10% government tax and 10% Service Charge 10% 税＋10% サービス料 別

HOTEL DU PALAIS
Biarritz, France

オテル・デュ・パレ
ビアリッツ　フランス

042

フランス南西部にある街・ビアリッツ。そこに、オテル・デュ・パレはある。フランスには5つ星ホテルを超えるカテゴリーとして「パラス」（Palace）というものがある。2013年6月にパリのロイヤル・モンソー（当旅行ガイドシリーズ3弾「バル・タパス・アルサック」で紹介済）が認定されても、まだわずか13軒のホテルだけだが、オテル・デュ・パレは最初にパラスに認定されたホテルの一つだ。

HOTEL DU PALAIS is located in Biarritz, France. It is ranked as "Palace", a special category above 5-star, by French government. Only 13 hotels have obtained the award so far. The Royal Monceau, Paris, introduced in my previous travel guide "Bar, Tapas, & Arzak", was the last one.

落ち着いた雰囲気の、手入れが行き届いた客室。
You can relux in the rooms with a peaceful atmosphere.

ナポレオンのNの家紋。We find Napoleon's "N".

大西洋とビーチを見下ろすオテル・デュ・パレは、元々はナポレオン三世とその妻ウジェニーの夏の別荘だった。それをビアリッツ市が購入し、古き良き昔の佇まいを丁寧に修理し生かしながら、近代的設備な設備に改装している。

　バスク地方は、サンセバスチャンやビルバオに代表されるスペイン北部と、バイヨンヌやここビアリッツに代表される南西フランスにまたがる七つのエリアから構成される。オテル・デュ・パレは南西フランスのバスク地方に位置する。ホテルの周辺にはバスク地方特有の豊かな自然がある。

HOTEL DU PALAIS, which has a good view of the Atlantic Ocean and the beach, was originally the summer house for The Napolean III and his wife, Eugenie. Later Biarritz city purchased the house and changed it into a hotel with great care over a long time.

　Basque country consists of seven areas in the North of Spain, which has San Sebastian and Bilbao, and the Southwest France, which has Biarritz and Bayonne. This Hotel Du Palais is located in the Southwest France side and it has a rich Basque heritage.

水回りは新しい。Bathrooms are new.

045

バスクの新鮮な素材を楽しむ。
Enjoy the very fresh local food there.

シェフのジーン・マリー・ゴーティエさんは多くの料理人を育てた「先生」として尊敬されている。
The chef, Mr. Jean-Marie Gautier, has brought up many young chefs and he is respected as a great teacher.

ミシュラン1つ星のレストラン・ヴィラ・ウジェニーでは、料理の素材の新鮮な味に驚かされる。
Villa Eugenie, with one Michelin star, serves delicious dishes with very fresh local food.

ホテルから徒歩約15分のところにマルシェがある。
Around 15 minutes walk from the hotel takes you to Marche in the city.

新鮮な牡蠣は美味。
You can taste very fresh oysters.

バスクと言えばバカラオ（干しだら）。
Bacalao looks tasty.

マルシェのカフェで休憩。
Relax at the cafes around the market.

マルシェ内のこのチーズ屋さんはすごい。
This cheese shop in Marche is so great.

チーズ好きでなくても夢中になるほど美味。
I went crasy with the cheese, even though I don't like cheese much.

この唐辛子ジャムがチーズに合う。
The chili jam makes cheese more delicious.

049

マルシェから車で5分のところに、ミシュラン一つ星のレストラン「レ・ロジェ」がある。
"Les Rosiers" is a restaurant with one Michelin star five minutes from Marche.

レ・ロジェのシェフ、アンドレ
Andree, the Chef of Les Rosiers

　　オテル・デュ・パレから程近いところにある、ミシュラン1つ星のレストラン「レ・ロジェ」のシェフ、アンドレ・ロジェは女性で初めてフランス国家最優秀職人賞を受賞したシェフ。彼女もP46で紹介したホテルのシェフ・ジーンさんの教え子だ。彼女がタダモノでないことは料理を一口食べればわかる。おいしさがシャープだ。

The Chef of Les Rosiers, Andree Rosiers, is the first female chef to receive M.O.F. (Meilleur Ouvrier de France). She is one of the "students" taught by the Chef of Hotel Du Palais, Jean-Marie Gautier.

051

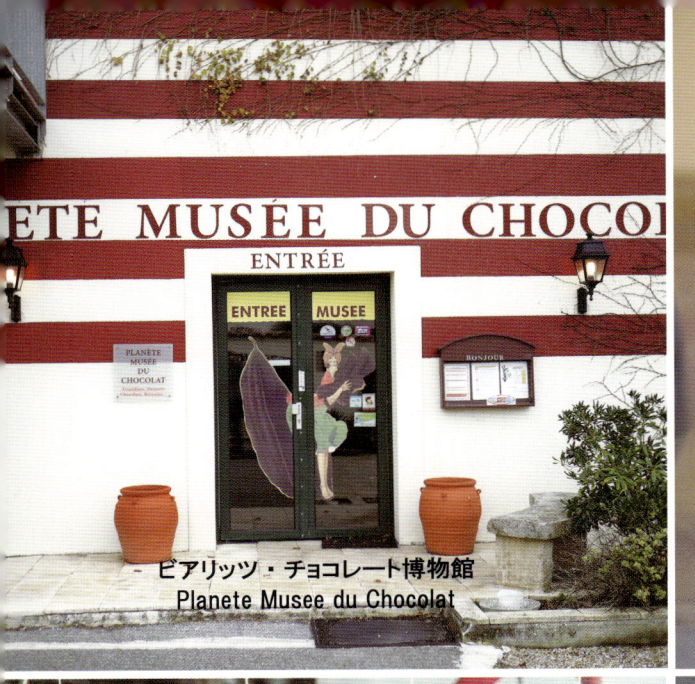

ビアリッツ・チョコレート博物館
Planete Musee du Chocolat

チョコレートがヨーロッパに伝わる歴史を知る
The museum shows us the histry of chocolate in Europe.

バスクと言えば唐辛子。どの軒先にも干してある。
Each house dries red chili on their window

バスク織のデザインにも唐辛子。
Basque linen also has the design of red chili.

052

HOTEL DU PALAIS オテル・デュ・パレ

URL： http://www.hotel-du-palais.com
Email: reception@hotel-du-palais.com ＊英語・フランス語のみ
Tel： ++33 (0)5 59 41 64 00
Rates 料金：Prestige Ocean View Room Euro 750〜 (Subject to changes)
＊日本円で約 10.5 万円（＋税・サ別）
（1 Euro ＝約 140 円（2014年7月21日現在）で計算

LISBON

Portugal

ポルトガル　リスボン

サンタジェスタのエレベーターからの街並み
The view from Sant Justa Lift

054

リスボンの旧市街の真ん中にあるサンタジェスタのエレベーター
Sant Justa Lift is located at the center of the old town of Lisbon.

ポルトガルの首都・リスボンは、昔ながらの街並みが残り、食事もお酒もおいしく、物価も安い楽しい街だ。ワインも楽しめる。微発泡のヴィーニョ・ヴェルデ（Vinho Verde）、有名なポートワイン、マデイラワインなどなど楽しみが多い。

Lisbon is a very attractive city with beautiful views of old style buildings and delicious foods at reasonable prices. Tasting the loca wines like Vinho Verde, Port, and Madeira is espeicially fun.

055

コメルシオ広場のジョゼ1世騎馬像
King Jose I Statue
at Paraca do Comerico (Commerce Square)
Photo taken by Taiyo Ishii

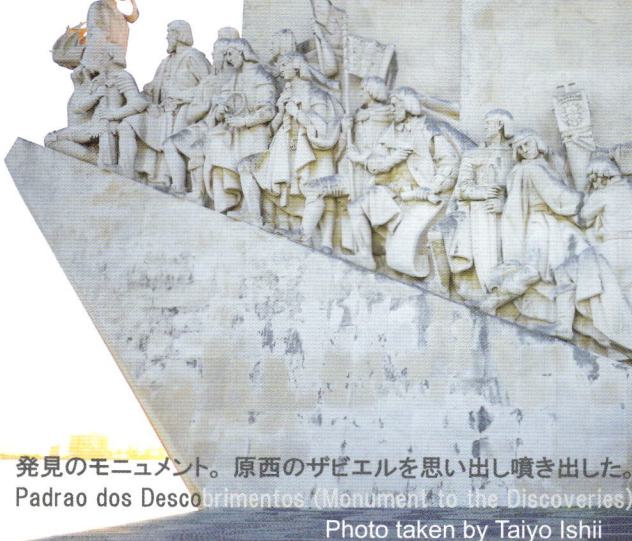

発見のモニュメント。原西のザビエルを思い出し噴き出した。
Padrao dos Descobrimentos (Monument to the Discoveries)
Photo taken by Taiyo Ishii

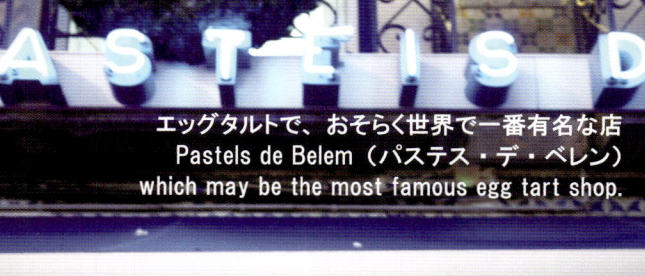

エッグタルトで、おそらく世界で一番有名な店
Pastels de Belem（パステス・デ・ベレン）
which may be the most famous egg tart shop.
Photo taken by Taiyo Ishii

このパステル・デ・ナタは、おそらく読者が想像している味と違う。
The taste of this Pastel de Nata may be different from what you imagine.
Photo taken by Taiyo Ishii

サンニコラウ通りにあるセレクトショップ
A sophisticated shop which sells handmade Portuguese items.

アンティークなタイルなどもある
The shop located at Rua de Sao Nicolau has antique ceramics, too.

リスボンには、小さ　がおいしい　店がある。
"Taberna da Rua das Flores" is a tiny restaurant.

タベルナ・ダル・ア・ダス・フロレスは
おいしい料理が手ごろな料金で、接客も気持ち良い。
The "taberna" has many delicious dishes and local wines with reasonable price.

FEITORIA
Lisbon, Portugal

2種類のバターやオリーブオイルは、ポルトガルの異なる産地のもので、まったく味が異なることに驚く。
Two kinds of olive oils and butters from the different regions in Portugal, which have very different tastes and flavors.

リスボンに来たら、ぜひ立ち寄ってほしいのが、このフェイトリアというレストランだ。ミシュラン1つ星。フェイトリアという言葉は英語のFactoryに該当するポルトガル語だ。第一義は「工場」だが、「在外商館」の意味もある。つまり、大航海時代以降、日本の長崎の出島のような在外商館は、海外に接することができる数少ない場所だった。フェイトリアでは、ポルトガルの地元の食材を使い、海外のフレーバーを取り入れた洗練された料理を味わうことができる。

You should experience this restaurant, which has one Michelin star, when you visit Lisbon. A Portuguese word "Feitoria" is equivalent to "Factory" in English. The word sometimes means a commercial house out side of the country in the Golden Age of Discovery. You will enjy the sophisticated dishes made from the local fresh produce with cooked with international methods and flavors.

オレンジとサーモンのマカロン
Orange and Salmon macaroon, one of the Chef Aperitifs

タラのコンフィ。だしを注ぐ。
Cod fish confit, another of the Chef Aperitifs

洗練された内装
Cozy interior and atmosphere

シェフのジョアオ・ロドリゲス（左から2番目）とチーム
The Chef, Joao Rodrigues, the 2nd from the left, and his team

FEITORIA フェイトリア
URL： http://www.restaurantefeitoria.com/
Email： reservationsbelem@altishotels.com
Tel： +351 210 400 200
Rates 料金：**5 course tasting menu Euro 120~** (beverage not included)
　　　＊日本円で約 16,800 円（＋税・サ別）
　　　　（1 Euro ＝約 140 円（2014年7月21日現在）で計算

The HALKIN by COMO, London

ひと言で言うと、私好みのホテルだ。新しいがシック。洗練されている。こじんまりとしていて落ち着いた雰囲気。立地もロンドンの中心地・ハイド・パーク・コーナーのそばで便利。でも、静かなエリア。スタッフの対応もフレンドリーで、かつ、スピーディー。あとで紹介する、抜群においしいレストラン（AMESTA）もある。なかなかこれ以上のホテルをロンドンで探すのは難しいかも、と素朴に思う素晴らしいホテルだ。唯一の難点と言えば、41室しかないので、予約をとるのが大変などころだろうか。とにかく、次回ロンドンに滞在するときにはぜひお試しに宿泊してみてほしい。

In a word, The Halkin by COMO, London, is my favourite hotel. It is chic, sophisticated, cozy, and small. The hotel is located near Hyde Park Corner, the centre of London, in a residential area. The staff are friendly and efficient. It has one of the best restaurants in London, Ametsa, introduced from page 66 in this guide. I simply think that it is difficult to find any better boutique hotel in London than The Halkin by COMO. With just 41 bedrooms, I recommend making reservations in advance for your next London visit.

シックで上質な室内
The interior is chic and of high quality.

THE HALKIN

5-6 HALKIN STREET

064

The HALKIN by COMO, London
ザ・ハルキン・バイ・コモ・ロンドン

URL： http://www.comohotels.com/thehalkin/
Email： thehalkin@comohotels.com
Tel： +44 (0) 20 7333 1000
Rates 料金：Superior Room GBP 330~ (plus taxes and fees)
　＊日本円で約 56,100 円（＋税・サ別。1GBP ポンド ＝約 170 円（2014年7月現在）で計算

Amesta
with Arzak Instruction

壁にかけられた写真は、バスクの彫刻家エドアルド・チリダの作品「風のトサカ」。
The photo on the wall is "Wind's comb" by Eduardo Chillida, a basque sculptor.

前菜の一つ。ホタテとキャッサバのスフレ
One of "Entrantes". Scallops with Cassava "Souffle"

アメスタは、前ページまでで紹介したザ・ハルキンの中にあるレストランだ。スペイン北部の町・サンセバスチャンにある三ツ星レストラン「アルサック」のエレーナ・アルサック率いるチームのプロデュースによる。世界を席巻しているヌエバ・コシーナ・バスカ（新バスク料理）をロンドンで味わえる。お勧めはディナー・テイスティング・メニューだ。5種類のグラスワインとのペアリングとあわせて145ポンド（約2万5千円）の料金だ。今はまだミシュラン1つ星だが、個人的には、こんなおいしい料理は久々に食べたというくらいおいしかった。内装はモダン。ABロジャーズ・デザインによる。

Amesta, located in The Halkin by COMO, introduced here from page 62, is a one Michelin star restaurant, spearheaded by Elena Arzak, who also runs "Arzak" the three Michelin star restaurant in San Sebastian, North Spain. Since it's opening, you can now enjoy classic "Nueva Cocina Vasca" in London. I recommend guests to choose the "dinner tasting menu" with wine parings (5 glasses of wines), priced at GBP145. My personal impression was that I had never enjoyed such a delicious dinner ever. The interior here is modern, designed by London-based interior designer AB Rogers design. The restaurant manager Godoy shows his exceptional leadership in all aspects of the guest experience.

マトウダイのビーツ風味モホソース
（パンとナッツのソース）
Johe Dory with Red Root "Mojo"

067

前菜の盛り合わせ
Aperitovos,
Cod Skin with Green Basque Chilli Pepper
and Tomato with Iberico Ham

エビとクモ蟹、バーミチェリとスイートコーン添え
King Prawns and Spider Crab
with Vermicelli and Sweet Corn

ロブスターとホワイト・オリーブオイル
Lobster with White Olive Oil

玉子とカバ（プレデザート）
Egg with Cava, the Pre-dessert

069

調理場のスタッフ　The chef and his team

マンザニアも料理にあわせて登場する
Manzanilla matches basqe dishes

モダンな内装
Modern interior designed by
London-based Ab Rogers Design

Amesta with Arzak Instruction
アメスタ・ウィズ・アルサック・インストラクション
URL ： http://www.comohotels.com/thehalkin/dining/ametsa
Tel ： +44 (0) 20 7333 1234
Rates 料金: Dinner Tasting Menu with Wine Paring GBP 145 (plus taxes and fees)
＊ 日本円で約 25,000 円（＋税・サ別。1GBP ポンド ＝約 170 円（2014年7月現在）で計算

Albania アルバニア

アルバニアの首都・ティラナから約20kmにあるクルヤ。
15世紀のバザールの街並みが残る。
お土産を買うのに最適な場所
Kruka, 20 km away from Tirana, the capital of Albania.
It has Derexhik Barrar, one of the typical bazaars
from the 15th centruy.

アルバニアの首都ティラナ誕生の父・スレイマン・パシャ
ティラナは2014年で誕生から400周年を迎える。
Sulekma Pasha Bargjini, the founder of Tirana.
2014 is the 400 years anniversary for Tirana as a city.

What idea do you have, when you hear the name of the country "Albania"? It has many beautiful places and ineteresting history episodes. For example, Shkodra, a city in th North, has the breathtaking view from Rozafa Castle. And, "Bas-relief of Rozafa", the bas-relief of a young mother giving only one breast to feed her little baby, has an interesting legend. In this travelguide, however, I introduce many delicious Albanian dishes.

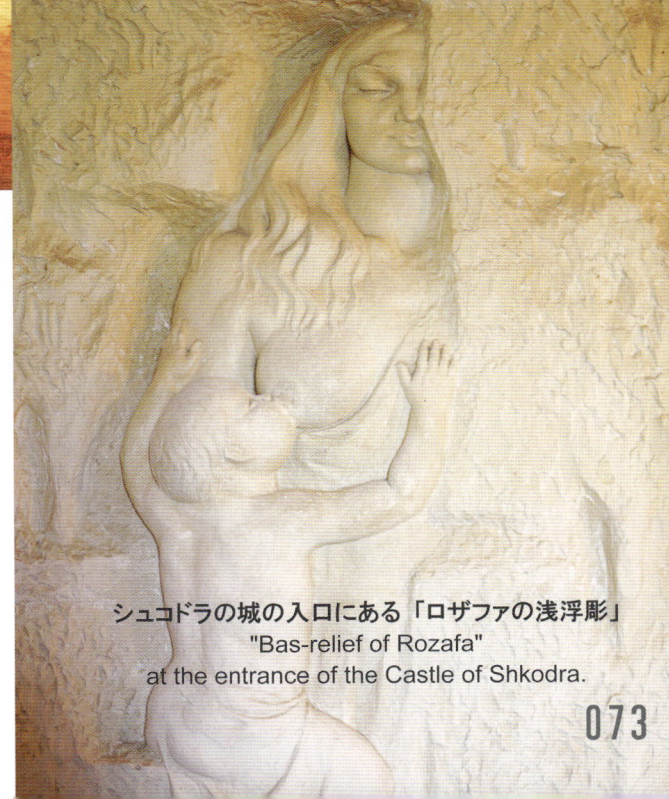

アルバニアと訊いてイメージが湧く日本人は少数だろう。ありきたりの行き先に飽きた人には、美しい景色と興味深い歴史があるアルバニアはお勧めだ。例えばアルバニア北部の街・シュコドラのロザファ城からの景色は素晴らしい。また、城の入口にある「ロザファの浅浮彫」は印象的だ（右写真）。描かれている若い母親の片方の乳と腕だけが赤ちゃんに与えられ、もう片方は壁に埋もれている。城を敵から守るために若い母親が壁に閉じ込められたという伝説だ。

このガイドで食道楽の私が紹介するのは、アルバニアの料理だ。ギリシャ料理あるいはバルカン半島の料理とも一味違うアルバニアの料理を紹介しよう。

シュコドラの城の入口にある「ロザファの浅浮彫」
"Bas-relief of Rozafa"
at the entrance of the Castle of Shkodra.

073

アルバニアの伝統料理のひとつ コーンブレッド。
ヨーグルトをかけて食べる。
Cornbread with Yogurt, a typical Albanan traditional food

ティラナにあるアルバニア伝統料理の店「サラベト」
Sarabet, a restaurant with traditional Albanian foods in Tirana
www.sarajet.com

ヤギの乳のチーズのオーブン焼き
意外とクセがなくおいしい
Baked goat cheese in Oven

シュコドラのレストラン「トラディタ・トスケ」
"Tradita Toske dhe Gege" in Shkodra
http://www.hoteltradita.com/restaurant/

北部の町・レジャにあるレストラン「ムリジ・ザナベ」
将来ミシュランの星、間違いなし！
Restaurant "Mrizi Zanave" in Fishte, in Zadrima region.
I am sure Mrizi will get Michelin stars in the future.
http://www.mrizizanave.com/mrizi/

白トリュフのリゾット
White Truffle resotto

075

ティラナにあるアルバニア伝統料理の店「オダ」
オスマントルコの伝統料理を楽しめる。
"Oda", Ottoman-style in a true traditional restaurant in Tirana
Open 11:00-23:00, Sun 13:00-23:00.
Address: Rr. Luigj Gurakuqi, Tirana
Phone: +355 4 224 95 41

揚げおにぎり「キフキ」
"Qifqi", a fried rice ball traditional in South Albania

リーキ（西洋ネギ）のパイ「パカロク」
"Pacarok", a traditional leek pie

店内ではオスマントルコ伝統の
低い椅子とテーブルで食事をする。
店名のOdaはアルバニア語で「客間」の意味。

Sitting on ottoman stools at low tables in Oda, which means "guest room" in Albanian language.

アルバニアのグラッパ「ラキ」。オダでは自家製だ。
You enjoy Raki, a traditional fruit brandy in Albania.

Raki Manaferre 2005

アルバニアのホテルを紹介しよう。
首都ティラナの気持ちの良いテラスがある「ログネル・ホテル・ティラナ」
バスタブはないが、シャワーだけでOKの人なら快適なホテルだ。
Rogner Hotel Tirana, which has a sunny comfortable terrace.
http://hotel-europapark.com/

ハズレなし。「シェラトン・ティラナ・ホテル」
The same anywahere in the world,
"Sheraton Tirana Hotel"
http://www.sheratontiranahotel.com/

ティラナの4つ星、モンディアル・ホテル
クラシックなデザインだがエアコンなどは日本製だ。
4-star hotel in Tirana, "Mondial Hotel"
Clasical design with modern facilitis.
http://www.hotelmondial.com.al

個人的にはお気に入り。「チェコ・インペリアル」
My personal favorite, "XHEKOO IMPERIAL"
http://www.xheko-imperial.com/en/

アルバニアで最も有名なデュレス・ビーチのホテル
ホテル・アドリアティク。目の前にはアドレナ海が広がる
Hotel Adriatik, A resort hotel in Durres Beach,
the most popular beach in Albania.
http://www.adriatikhotel.com/

079

Song Saa Private Island, Cambodia

カンボジアは、食に関して日本と古くからの縁がある国だ。たとえば「かぼちゃ」。かぼちゃはカンボジアの産物として伝来したことから、カンボジアが訛って「かぼちゃ」になったとされている。「うどん」もカンボジアのウドンという町で食されていた麺が由来だという説がある。新鮮な食材に恵まれた、旧フランス領のカンボジアは食事がおいしい。ここ「ソンサー・プライベート・アイランド」（以下、ソンサー）は私にとっては忘れられない食の思い出の場所だ。ソンサーはカンボジアにある一島一リゾートのプライベート・アイランドだ。オールインクルッシブのリゾートだから、一部のワインなどを除いて、飲食はすべて宿泊代に含まれている。

Cambodia is a country with a long relationship with Japan in terms of food. For exmaple, pumpkin is called "Kabocha" in Japanese language. Because pumpkin was brought to Japan as a product of Cambodia, the name was named after the pronunciation of Cambodia. Udon noodle, too. It is said that Udon noodle is named after a town of "Oudong". The foods of Cambodia, which used to be an old French territory, are delicious. For me, the foods I had in Song Saa Private Island ("Song Saa") are unforgettable. It is an all-inclusive resort, so that most foods and bevarages are included in the fare.

部屋についたインフィニティ・プール
Private infinity pool at a room

ソンサーまではスピードボートで移動
This speed boat takes you to Song Saa.

カンボジア名産の房成りの胡椒が甘い。
Cambodian pepper corn is so sweet.

プノンペン国際空港から南部のシアヌークビルまで車で3時間。そこからスピードボートで約30分でソンサーに到着する。ソンサーでの一番のお勧めは、隣島のコーロン島のファイブ・マイル・ビーチでのピクニック・ランチだ。私の好物は、房成りの胡椒とビーフのソテー。フレッシュな胡椒の甘さがクセになる。

A 3-hour drive takes you to from Phnom Penh international airport, Sihanoukville, and it takes 30 minutes in the resort's speed boat to Song Saa. My favorite food there is the picnic lunch, served at Five Mile Beach at Koron island, the island next to the resort. Fresh Cambodian pepper corn is so sweet.

嫌なことをすべて忘れられる天国の一瞬
The heavenly moment when you can forget everything.

ノム・バグン・チュク（メコン川の魚のすりおろしをかけたビーフン）
Noum Bagn Chuk
(Vermicelli rice noodles with Mekong Fish)

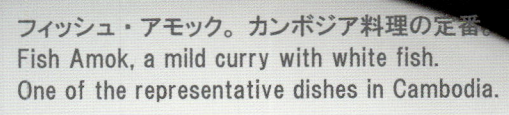

フィッシュ・アモック。カンボジア料理の定番。
Fish Amok, a mild curry with white fish.
One of the representative dishes in Cambodia.

プラホック。魚を発酵させた調味料。野菜のディップなどで食べる。日本人にとっての「味噌」のような存在。
Prahok, paste from permented fish.
The most typical seasoning in Cambodia.

Song Saa Private Island
ソンサー・プライベート・アイランド

URL： http://songsaa.com/
Tel： +855 236 860 360
E-mail： reservations@songsaa.com
Rates 料金：One bed room Ocean View from US$1,649 (plus taxes and fees)
*All inclusive basis（特別なワイン等を除いた飲食代込の値段）

＊日本円で約17万円（＋税・サ別。1GBP ポンド ＝約 103 円（2014年8月現在）で計算

Grand Hyatt Fukuoka
Japan

このシリーズで初めて日本のリゾートを紹介する。福岡は外国人旅行者に人気のある街だが、ここグランド ハイアット 福岡は、外国人が快適でかつ楽しい滞在を過ごせるベストの場所だと断言できる。なぜか。グランド ハイアットだから快適なのは当たり前。外国人に人気のスポット「キャナルシティ博多」に隣接し、中洲の屋台までも徒歩数分だからだ。

Here I introduce a Japanese resort for the first time in this travel guide series. Fukuoka is a popular destination for foreign tourists and I am sure that Grand Hyatt Fukuoka is the best place for international guests, because not only is the stay comfortable, but also you will have fun in the surrounding areas.

部屋が快適なのは言うまでもない。
Nice rooms are comfortable.

ホテルなのに日本式のお風呂。
The unique point of Grand Hyatt Fukuoka is that they have Japanese style baths in all the rooms. You wash your body in the area next to the bathtub. You take a seat on the stool and clean your body with soap.

長い光るバーカウンター
The long and shining bar counter

25mプール、2種類のサウナもあるスパ・フィットネスクラブ「クラブ オリンパス」。もちろんトリートメントも充実。
Spa/fitness club "Club Olympus" has 25-meter swimming pool, two kinds of Sauna and fitness equipment.

ホテルと隣接する「キャナルシティ博多」の間のエリアで、迫力ある噴水が見られる。
We enjoy the great fountain show in an area between the hotel and "Canal City Hakata",
a shopping mall complex next to the hotel.

089

キャナルシティ博多には外国人観光客が喜ぶところがたくさん。
Canal City Hakata has many fun places for foreign tourists.

ホテルから徒歩数分のところには屋台がある。
A few minutes walk takes you to Yatai, food stand shops.

Grand Hyatt Fukuoka
グランド ハイアット 福岡

URL： http://fukuoka.grand.hyatt.jp/
Tel： 092 282 1234
E-mail： fukuoka.grand@hyatt.com
Rates 料金：クラブキング（2名1室）35,000 円〜（消費税別）
*Club King for 2 persons JPY 32,200, about US$ 340 〜
*1 US$ = JPY 103 (as of Aug 2014)

091

Ocean Suites
Resort World Sentosa
Singapore

水族館の紹介をしているわけではない。左の写真は、実は客室の窓からの景色だ。なんと窓のシェードを開けると、そこには魚が泳いでいる。シンガポール・セントーサ島のリゾート・ワールド・セントーサ（以下、リゾート・ワールド）にあるオーシャン・スイーツという特別なホテルだ。リゾート・ワールドは子連れファミリーには最高の場所だ。ユニバーサル・スタジオや世界最大の水族館のシー・アクアリウムがある。その水族館のプールに対面してホテルの部屋を作った。わずか11室だけの特別なホテルだ。各部屋はメゾネットになっていて、上階は水面の上にあり、下階が水面下となっている。

11のスイートが並ぶ。
11 suite rooms are in a line.

上階がリビングエリア。
The upper level is a living area.

I am not introducing an aquarium. The photo in the left page is the view from the window of the guest room. When you open the shade of the window, you find many fish swimming. This is the special hotel "Ocean Suites" in Rosorts World Sentosa ("Resorts World"), Sentosa, Singapore. Resorts World is the best place to visit with small kids. It has Universal Studio and S.E.A Aquarium, the largest aquarium in the world. This special hotel is built for the widows in front of the aquarium's pool. There are 11 exlusive suites only, which have an upper level with outdoore patio and Jacuzzi.

アクエリアス・ホテルのバー
The bar at Equarius Hotel

リゾート・ワールドには、このオーシャン・スイートの他に、ハードロック・ホテル・シンガポール、フェスティブ・ホテル、ホテル・マイケル、エクアリアス・ホテル、ビーチ・ヴィラ、ツリー・トップ・ロフトと6つのホテルがある。それぞれ個性あふれるホテルだ。たとえばツリー・トップ・ロフトはわずか2棟のみだが、木立ちの中の地上12メートルの高さにひそくと立つ隠れ家的なホテルだ。オーシャン・スイートは、位置的にはエクアリアス・ホテルの地下にあり、ロビーや朝食のレストランなどはエクアリアス・ホテルと共通になる。エクアリアス・ホテルはナチュラル・テイストのデザインで統一されている。

Resort World has 6 hotels apart from Ocean Suites: Hard Rock Hotel, Festive Hotel, Hotel Michael, Equarius Hotel, Beach Villas, and TreeTop Lofts. Each hotel has a totally different atmosphere. For exmaple, at TreeTop Lofts, two one-bedroom lofts are perched at 12 meters high in the trees. In terms of location, Ocean Suites is at the basement of Equarius Hotel, the design of which is with natural taste. The guests in Ocean Suites use the lobby and breakfast restaurant of Equarius Hotel.

落ち着いた雰囲気のアクエリアスホテル
Equarius Hotel has a calm atmosphere.

オーシャン・スイートでは湯船からこの景色を楽しめる。
You enjoy this view from the bathtub in Ocean Suites.

アクエリアスホテルのレストラン・フォレスト
Forest, a restaurant in Equarius Hotel

看板はまさに「森」
森 means Forest in Chinese and Japanese.

点心の種類歩が豊富
Many kinds of dim sum there.

日本人にはなじみがない上海パンケーキ
Shanghai Pancake, new for Japanese people

オーシャン・スイートの朝食会場は、アクエリアス・ホテルのレストラン「フォレスト」だ。点心やフルーツが充実している。夜は創作中華になる。また、まさに部屋と同じように水族館の魚を窓越しに見ながら食事ができるオーシャン・レストランは部屋の並びにある。そこの米国人シェフ、キャット・コーラはアメリカ版「料理の鉄人」女性初めてのの鉄人とのこと。

Breakfast is served at the restaurant "Forest" in Equarius hotel. Ocean Suites has a different restaurant for dinner, "Ocean Restaurant by Cat Cora" next to the suites in the basement. The chef Cat Cora was the fist lady Iron chef in a TV program in U.S.

ESPA（エスパ）にはハマムもある。
ESPA has a Hammam, too.
© Resorts World at Sentosa Pte. Ltd. All Rights Reserved

素晴らしい景色の開放的な空間
Enjoy the spectacular view in secluded space.
© Resorts World at Sentosa Pte. Ltd. All Rights Reserved

ベッドルームも広い。
The bedrooms in Beach Villas are spacious.

リゾート・ワールドにあるもう一つのゴージャスな宿泊場所はビーチ・ビラだ。素晴らしい景色を楽しみながら、開放的だがプライベートな空間でゆったりと過ごせる。また、ビーチ・ビラの宿泊者は世界的に有名なスパESPAのサウナ、ハマム、バイタリティ・プールなどを利用することができる。

Beach Villas, another luxury hotel in Resort World, has spectacular view and peaceful atmosphere in the private area. The guest staying at Baech Villas have access to the facilities iike two kinds of saunas, Hammam, and outdoor vitality pool and cold plunge pool.

Ocean Suites, World Resort Sentosa
オーシャン・スイート（ワールド・リゾート・セントーサ）

URL： http://www.rwsentosa.com/
　　　＊予約は「ビーチ・ビラ」の「オーシャン・スイート」を選ぶ
Tel： + 65 6577 8888
E-mail： reservation@rwsentosa.com
Rates 料金： Ocean Suite　SG$1765.5〜 (plus taxes and fees)
　　　＊オーシャン・スイート　1765.5シンガポールドル〜(税・手数料別)
　　　＊1シンガポールドル = 82円 (2014年8月現在) の換算で約14万5千円

Belmond Governor's Residence
Yangon
Myanmar

ベルモンド・ガバナーズ・レジデンスは、1920年代のコロニアル調の大邸宅を利用したホテルだ。シュエダゴン・パゴダという2500年前からの大寺院から程近い、ヤンゴンの大使館地区にある。穏やかな南国の風を感じながらの滞在は、初めてでも、とにかくリラックスできる。

The 1920's colonial style mansion in embassy area in Yangon is Belmond Governor's Residence. Shwedagon Pagoda, the landmark temple with 2,500 years' histry in Yangon, is not far from the resort. The calm tropical wind gives you instant relux even on your first visit.

歓迎のドラ。ホテルに到着すると鳴らしてくれる。
Welcome gong when you arrive at the resort.

落ち着いた雰囲気の客室
Guest room with balmy atmosphere

テラゾで作った大きな湯船でリラックス
A big bathtub made from terrazzo

とりわけ中年以降の日本人は、バスタブに浸からないとお風呂に入った感じがしないが、ここベルモンド・ガバナーズ・レジデンスには、テラゾで作った大きなバスタブがある。建物自体は100年近い歴史を持つが、たっぷりと使えるお湯も含めて、設備は現代的で快適だ。

Japanese people, especially above middle age, need to take a bath in bathtab. This resort has the traditional Myanmar style large bathtab made from terrazzo. The resort building itself has about 100 years' history, but the eqiupment is very modern and comfortable.

南国の香りの風を感じる
You feel the tropical fragrances in the wind.

ミャンマーの伝統的なパンケーキ
Traditional Myanmar Pancake

スネーク・フルーツ
Snake fruit

ミャンマーの伝統的な朝食・モヒンガー
Mohingha, a traditional breakfast soup in Myanmar

ベルモンド・ガバナーズ・レジデンスの朝食はおいしい。朝食のブッフェでは普通の朝食メニューもあるが、ミャンマーの伝統的な朝食も担当できる。モヒンガーという麺は日本人の口に合う。スネーク・フルーツは東南アジアに見かけるフルーツだが、風船ガムのような変わった味がする。

The breakfast at the resort is very delicious. They serve not only normal hotel breakfast buffet, but also Myanmar traditional breakfast. I like Mohingha very much. I am sure that Japanese people will like the taste. Snake fruit, founded across South East Asia, tastes like bubble gum.

見ていると声を掛けられ、お願いするとモヒンガーを作ってくれる。女性の頬に塗ってあるのが有名なタナカ。
The female chef makes Mohingha for you. The makeup on her face is the famous "Thanaka", a cosmetic paste made from tree bark.

お茶の漬物・ラペット（中央の緑色のもの）
Lahpet, tea leaf salad (green at the center)

ミャンマーの伝統的デザート・シュエインエ
Shwe Yin Aye, the traditional desert

シャン・ヌードルを目前で作ってくれる
Shan noodle cooked in front of you

夕食は「バーミーズ・カレー・テーブル」（BURMESE CURRY TABLE）というブッフェをお勧めする。ミャンマーのカレーは辛くないし、カレーだけでもたくさん種類がある。また、カレー以外にもミャンマーの伝統料理が楽しめる。お茶の葉を発酵させた漬物「ラペット」がデザートコーナーに置いてあるのには驚いたが、消化を助けるために食後に食べるのが典型的らしい。

I recommend you try the "Burmese Curry Table" dinner buffet. Curries in Myanmar are not hot but tasty with various flavours. You enjoy other traditional foods in Myanmar, too. Tea leaf salad called Lahpet is served with desert, because it helps your digestion.

Belmond Governor's Residence
ベルモンド・ガバナーズ・レジデンス
URL： http://www.belmond.com/governors-residence-yangon/
Tel： +95 1 229860
Email： reservations.tgr@belmond.com
Rates 料金：**Delux room　US$261～** (plus taxes and fees)
　　　＊デラックス・ルーム　約27,000円～(税・手数料別)
　　　＊1 US＄＝103円 (2014年8月現在)の換算

Editor's Choice

Bataan Nuclear Power Plant
バターン原子力発電所
Phlippines　フィリピン

http://www.napocor.gov.ph/index.php/bataan-nuclear-power-plant

マニラから車で約3時間。バターンには一度も稼働したことがない原子力発電所がある。見学ツアーもある。
Battan, about 3-hours from Manil, has a nuclear power plant which has never been activated. You can join the tour to see inside.

Editor's Choice

Almedaren Week
アルメダーレン・ウィーク
Gotland, Sweden
スウェーデン・ゴットランド島

http://www.almedalsveckan.info

毎年7月、スウェーデンの政党幹部がゴットランド島に集まり、市民に対してスピーチを行い、気軽に討論する機会がある。アルメダーレンウィークと呼ばれる。1986年に暗殺された故オロフ・パルメ首相が1968年に島民からの依頼でスピーチをしたのが始まりだ。

In July every year, almost every political party sends its senior politician to Gotland Island to talk and disucuss freely with general citizens. It began with Olof Palme, a formar prime minister who was killed in 1986, who visited Gotland and made a speech based on the request of the island people.

実際に著者も2013年に参加し、キリスト民主党党首のゴラン・ハグランド厚労大臣と気軽に話せた。
In fact, I attended in 2013 and met and talked freely with Mr. Goran Hugglund, the leader of the Christian Democrats of Sweden and the minister for health and social affairs in the country.

Editor's Choice

HIGHGATE CEMETRY, London
ハイゲート・セメトリー（ロンドン）

WORKERS OF ALL LANDS UNITE

カール・マルクスのお墓がロンドンのハイゲート・セメトリーにある。1848年発行のエンゲルスとの共著『共産党宣言』にある有名なスローガン「万国の労働者、団結せよ！」が墓に刻まれている。

Karl Marx is buried at the east cemetery of Highgate Cemetry. The political slogan "Workers of all lands, unite!" is one of the most famous slogans of communism. It is found in The Communist Manifesto (1848), by Karl Marx and Friedrich Engels.

URL: http://highgatecemetery.org/

KARL MARX

Editor's Choice

Caféé Odeon, Zurich
カフェ・オデオン（チューリヒh）

レーニンは1917年のロシア革命の勃発を聞き、スイス・チューリッヒからドイツを経由して4月にロシアに帰国した。チューリッヒにいたレーニンは、カフェ・オデオンに頻繁に通い、ダダイズムの創始者トリスタン・ツァラとも親交を深めた。カフェ・オデオンは当時より縮小されたが、当時と同じ場所にある。

Vladimir Lenin, after he knew the Russian revolution had happened in 1917, returned to Russia through Germany from Zurich, Switzerland. Lenin often went to Café Odeon and became friends with Tristan Tzara, the founder of Dada movement. Café Odeon has become small, but is still in the same place.

URL: http://www.odeon.ch/en/

Editor's Choice

Statue of Elisabeth, Geneva
エリザベート像（ジュネーブ）

1898年、スイス・ジュネーブを訪れていたオーストリア妃エリザベート（通称シシィ）は、イタリア人のアナーキスト、ルイジ・ルケーニによってレマン湖のほとりで暗殺された。暗殺前に宿泊していたホテル、ボー・リバージュの前にエリザベートの像がある。
The Austrian Empress, Elisabeth "Sisi" was killed by an Italian anarchist Luigi Lucheni in 1898 along Lake Leman. The statue is built in front of a hotel named "Beau-Rivage Geneva", where she stayed before she was assassinated.

IN MEMORIAM

ELISABETH IMPERATRICE D'AUTRICHE, REINE DE HONGRIE

112

予期せぬ恋のガセーラ（タマリット詩集（1936年））

誰ひとり　お前の腹の暗い木蓮の
香りがわかっていなかった。
誰ひとり　お前がお前の歯の間で
恋の雀蜂を苦しめていることを　知らなかった
…
　　　　　ロルカ詩集（小海永二訳）土曜美術社出版販売

Museo Casa Natal Federico García Lorca
Fuente Vaqueros, Spain

ガルシア・ロルカ生家記念館
（スペイン　フエンテ・バケロス）

//www.patronatogarcialorca.org

同じく1898年に、グラナダ近郊のフエンテ・バケロスで生まれた詩人ガルシア・ロルカは、1936年にスペイン内戦でグラナダにて死亡。38歳だった。
In 1898, by chance the same year that Sisi was assassinated in Geneva, Federico Garcia Lorca, a Spanish poet, was born in Fuente Vaqueros, near Granada, Spain. He was killed in the Spanish Civil War in Granada in 1936.

Editor's Choice

113

Editor's Choice

アルハンブラの名前の由来は、アラビア語で「赤い城塞」を意味する言葉らしい。1492年のレコンキスタ（失地回復）は、スペイン・グラナダのアルハンブラ宮殿が陥落することで終焉した。
The name of Alhanbra comes from an Arabic word meaning "Red Castle". The Alhanbra fell in 1942 and the Reconquista was completed in Granada, Spain.

The Alhambra, Granada, Spain
アルハンブラ宮殿（スペイン・グラナダ）

http://www.alhambradegranada.org/en/
※チケットは事前にWEBで購入することを強くお勧めする。

Editor's Choice

The Red Bus in Warsaw
ワルシャワの赤いバス（ポーランド）

カジミェシュ・ヴィンクラーが作詞し、ウワディスワフ・シュピルマンが作曲した「ワルシャワの赤いバス」という歌は、今でもポーランド国民に愛されている。シュピルマンが父親の思い出をつづった本が原作となって、映画「戦場のピアニスト」は制作されたと言われている。

"Czerwony autobus" (Red Bus) is one of the most popular songs in Poland. The lyrics was written by Kazimierz Winkler and the music was composed by Wladek Szpilman, whose book "The pianist" was the basis for the movie "The pianist".

Editor's Choice

Chefchaouen, Morocco
シャウエン（モロッコ）

シャウエンは「青い町」として有名だ。スペインでのレコンキスタの後、多くのモリスコが、ここに移住したと言われている。
Chefchauen (or simply Chauen) is famous for its buildings in shades of blue. Many Moriscos moved and settled here after the Spanish Reconquista in medieval times.

Photo taken by Taiyo Ishii

Editor's Choice

Oswald's house in Minsk, Belarus
ミンスクのオズワルドの家（ベラルーシ）

ケネディ大統領を暗殺した犯人だとされるオズワルドは、1960年代初めの数年間を今のベラルーシ（当時のソ連）のミンスクで過ごしたとされている。その家は、ロシア社会民主労働党（後のソ連共産党）第1回会議場博物館の向かいになる。

Lee Harvey Oswald, who is said to have assassinated President, J.F. Kennedy, lived in Minsk, Belarus, in the Soviet Union at the time for a couple of years in the early 1960's. The house is just in front of the Museum of 1st Congress of the Social Democratic Labor Party of Russia, in Minsk.

Editor's Choice

DO & CO Hotel Vienna
ドー・アンド・コー ホテル
（ウィーン・オーストリア）

http://www.docohotel.com/en/

オーストリア・ウィーンのど真ん中、シュテファン教会の目の前にあるドー・アンド・コーホテルは、その立地のみならず、洗練されたデザインで人気だ。
Do & CO Hotel Vienna, in front of St. Stephen Cathedral located at the center of Vienna, is one of the most popular hotels in Vienna, not only because of the location, but also because of the sophisticated design.

Editor's Choice

Hotel Sans Sucie Wien
ホテル・サン・スーシー・ウィーン
（ウィーン・オーストリア）

オーストリア・ウィーンの中心地・フォルクスシアターのそばに2012年にできた新しいこのホテルは、美しい内装と、おいしい料理で満足すること請け合いだ。

Hotel Sans Sucie Wien, which opened in 2012 and is located near the Volkstheater, gives you beautiful rooms and delicious food. I am sure you will be satisfied.

http://www.sanssouci-wien.com/en

Editor's Choice

香港・セントラルのウエリントン・ストリートはＢ級グルメのメッカだ。
Wellington Streeet, Central, Hong Kong has many delicious reasonable noodles and dumplings..

王府の餃子 Dumplings at Wang Fu

沾仔記の鯪魚球麺
Fish Balls noodle at Tsim Chai Kee

Wellington Street, Hong Kong
ウエリントン・ストリート（香港・セントラル）

Wonton nuudle at Mak's Noodle
麥（不の下に大）雲吞麺世家の雲吞麺

Kenko Shokuhin Ramen
健康食品拉麺

Ho Chi Minh Museum (Bao Tang Ho Chi Minh)
Ho Chi Minh City, Vietnam
ホーチミン博物館
（ホーチミン・ベトナム）

日本語にも翻訳された詩集「獄中日記」の展示をはじめ、ベトナムを独立に導いたホー・チ・ミンの生涯を写真や資料で紹介。

The museum shows the life of Ho Chi Minh, who led the independence of Vietnam, with many interesting photos and materials including his poem book "Prison Poems".

http://www.baotanghochiminh-nr.vn/

Editor's Choice

Editor's Choice

Bogyoke Aung San Museum, Yangon, Myanmar
ボージョー・アウンサン博物館
（ミャンマー・ヤンゴン）

アウンサン・スーチーの父親のアウンサン将軍が、1947年に暗殺されるまでの最後の2年間を過ごした家が博物館になっている。
Bohyoke(General) Aung San Museum is the last house General Aung San lived at for two years before he was assassinated in 1947.

あとがき

「日本人のあまり行かない世界のセレブ・リゾート」シリーズはこの本で５冊目だ。今回は特に、何度も行っても楽しいところを紹介できていると思う。個人的には、ロンドンのレストラン・アメスタはお気に入りだ。今後、ミシュランの星の数がどんどん増えると予約も取りづらくなるし値段も高くなる。ロンドンは比較的行きやすいところだから、今のうちにぜひご来訪されたし。また、アルバニアやベラルーシなど、マイナーな旅先にも様々な発見がある。典型的な旅行先に飽きた人にはぜひお勧めだ。ご意見・ご感想は guide@ibcg.co.jp までお気軽にお送りください。

著者しるす

POSTSCRIPT

This is the 5th volume of the travel guide series named "Famous resorts for global rich celebrities, but unknown in Japan". I think this volume introduces many fun places to visit. I personally like Amesta, a restaurant in London, the best. They will have more Michelin stars, and it will become more difficult to make a reservation and more expensive. It's time to visit now. Here I introduce Albania and Beralus, which are not famous yet in Japan. But you will find something new there. If you're get bored with major destinations like New York and Paris, I recommend you to go to these new destinations. Your comment is welcome. "guide@ibcg.co.jp"

Itaru Ishii

CONTENTS

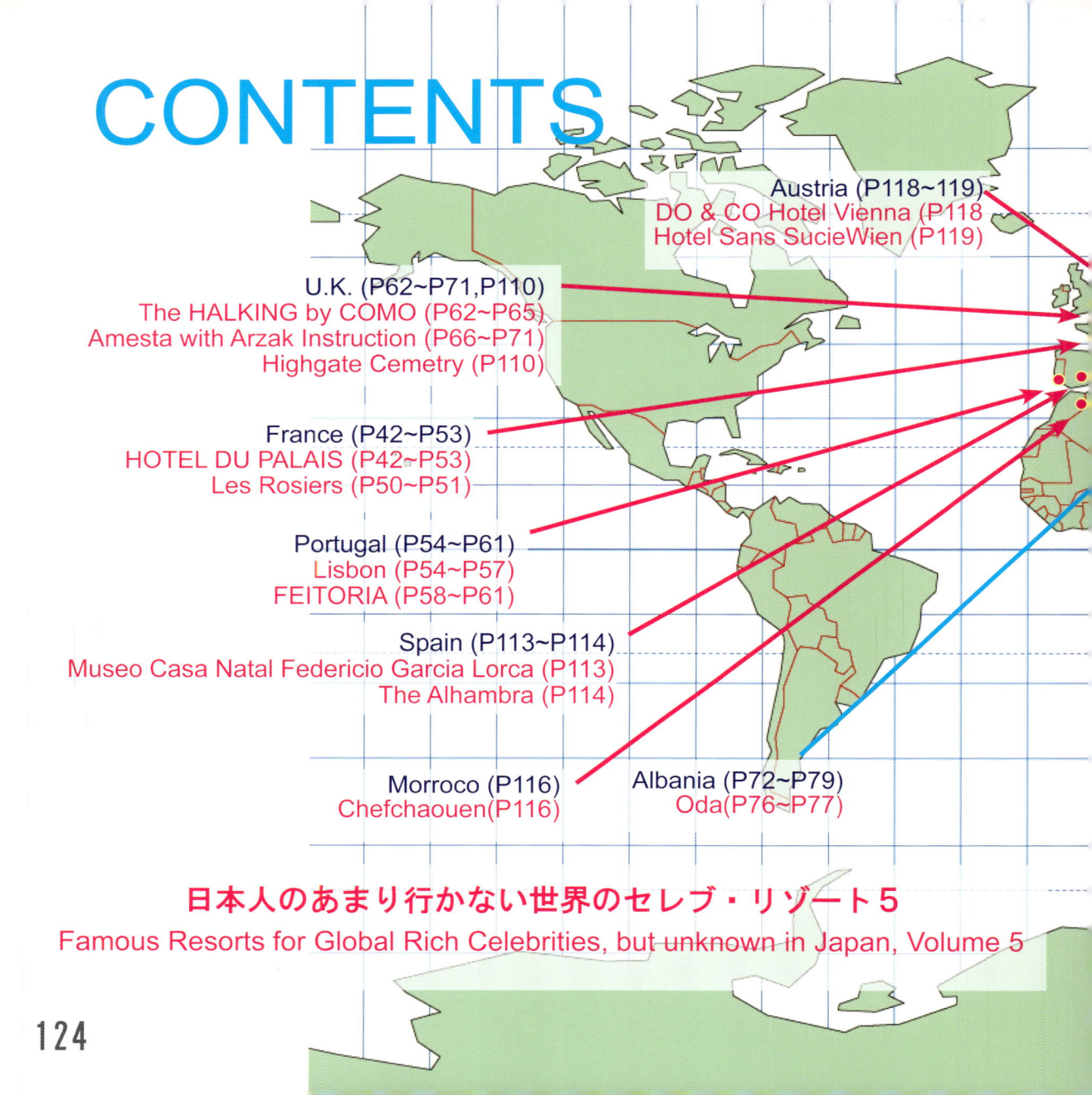

Austria (P118~P119)
DO & CO Hotel Vienna (P118
Hotel Sans SucieWien (P119)

U.K. (P62~P71,P110)
The HALKING by COMO (P62~P65)
Amesta with Arzak Instruction (P66~P71)
Highgate Cemetry (P110)

France (P42~P53)
HOTEL DU PALAIS (P42~P53)
Les Rosiers (P50~P51)

Portugal (P54~P61)
Lisbon (P54~P57)
FEITORIA (P58~P61)

Spain (P113~P114)
Museo Casa Natal Federicio Garcia Lorca (P113)
The Alhambra (P114)

Morroco (P116)
Chefchaouen(P116)

Albania (P72~P79)
Oda(P76~P77)

日本人のあまり行かない世界のセレブ・リゾート５
Famous Resorts for Global Rich Celebrities, but unknown in Japan, Volume 5

124

Sweden (P109)
Almedaren Week (P109)

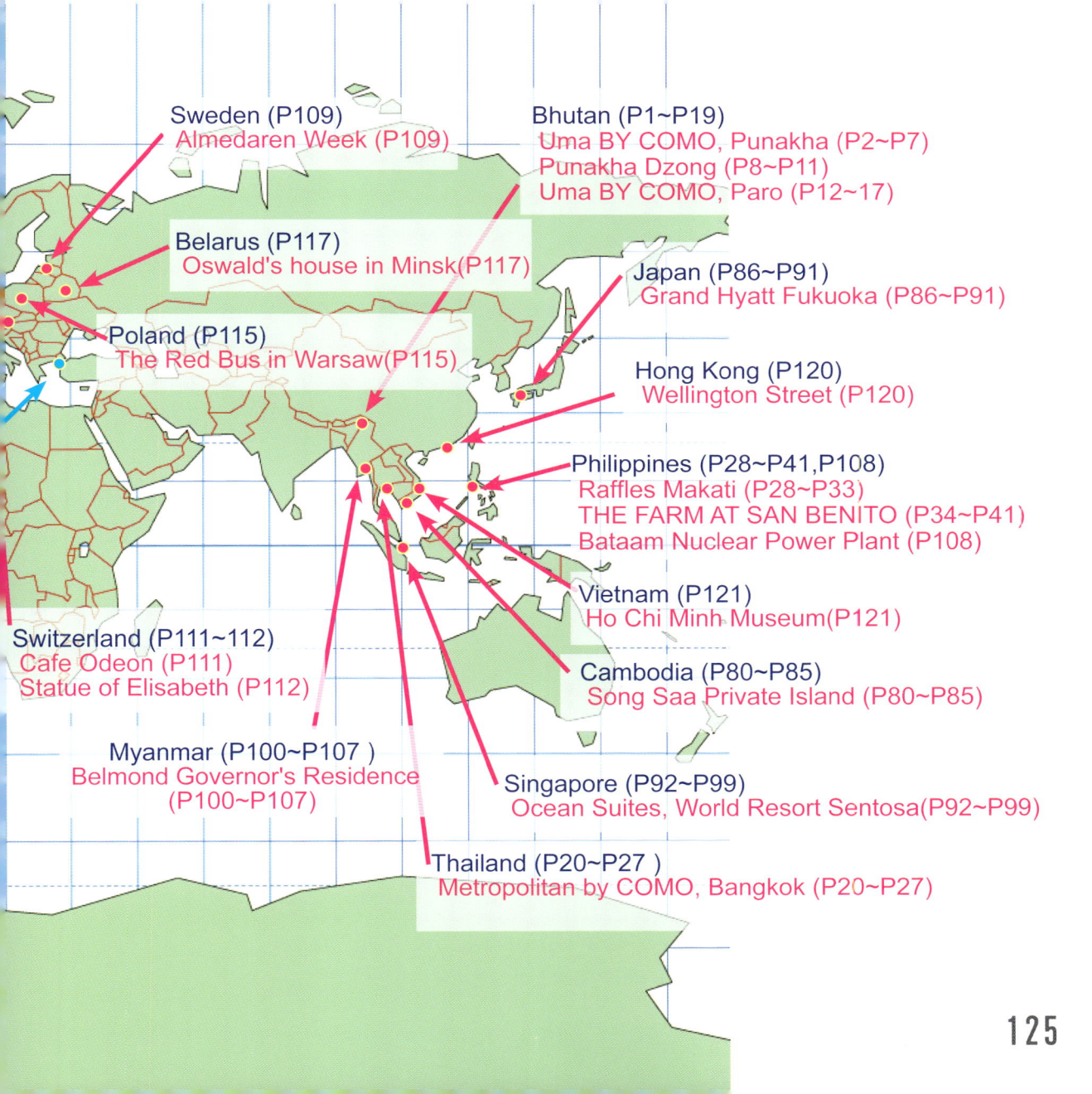

Bhutan (P1~P19)
Uma BY COMO, Punakha (P2~P7)
Punakha Dzong (P8~P11)
Uma BY COMO, Paro (P12~17)

Belarus (P117)
Oswald's house in Minsk(P117)

Japan (P86~P91)
Grand Hyatt Fukuoka (P86~P91)

Poland (P115)
The Red Bus in Warsaw(P115)

Hong Kong (P120)
Wellington Street (P120)

Philippines (P28~P41,P108)
Raffles Makati (P28~P33)
THE FARM AT SAN BENITO (P34~P41)
Bataam Nuclear Power Plant (P108)

Vietnam (P121)
Ho Chi Minh Museum(P121)

Switzerland (P111~112)
Cafe Odeon (P111)
Statue of Elisabeth (P112)

Cambodia (P80~P85)
Song Saa Private Island (P80~P85)

Myanmar (P100~P107)
Belmond Governor's Residence (P100~P107)

Singapore (P92~P99)
Ocean Suites, World Resort Sentosa(P92~P99)

Thailand (P20~P27)
Metropolitan by COMO, Bangkok (P20~P27)

マルクス、レーニン、ホー・チ・ミン
日本人のあまり行かない世界のセレブ・リゾート5

Marx, Lenin, and Ho Chi Minh
Famous Resorts for Global Rich Celebrities, but unknown in Japan, Volume 5

著者・写真（クレジット表記等がないもの）・編集
石井　至（いしい・いたる）観光立国推進有識者会議委員（2013年度、2014年度）。カンボジア観光省アドバイザー。1965年北海道生まれ。東京大学医学部卒。Ph.D.著書はこのシリーズの他、「グローバル資本主義を卒業した僕の選択と結論」（日経BP）、「慶應幼稚舎」（幻冬舎新書）、「慶応幼稚舎と慶應横浜初等部」（朝日新書）など多数。

Author /Photos(without credit) /Edit
Itaru Ishii, born in 1965 in Hokkaido, Japan. Graduated University of Tokyo, Faculty of Medicine. Ph.D. Member of Advisory Council on Tourism Nation Promotion of Japan (Apr2013~), Advisor to Minister of Tourism of Cambodia. He has over 40 books published, including this series, e.g. "My choice and Conclusion after I Graduated Global Capitalism" (Nikkei Business Publishing).

Special thanks to Mr. James Emmett.

2014年9月30日	初版第1刷発行	
著者	石井　至	
発行人	石井　至	
発行・販売	石井兄弟社（http://www.ibcg.co.jp）	
	〒150-0001　東京都渋谷区神宮前1-17-5-503	
	電話：03-5775-1385　FAX：03-5775-1386	
印刷・製本	株式会社シナノ書籍印刷	
ISBN	978-4-903852-11-9	

Printed in Japan
Copyright © 2014 Itaru Ishii, All right reserved
落丁・乱丁本はお取替えいたします。